ANTHROPOLOGICAL PAPERS

MUSEUM OF ANTHROPOLOGY, UNIVERSITY OF MICHIGAN

No. 4

Lumbar Breakdown Caused By Erect Posture In Man

With emphasis on Spondylolisthesis and
Herniated Intervertebral Discs

by
FREDERICK P. THIEME

ANN ARBOR
UNIVERSITY OF MICHIGAN PRESS, 1950

© 1950 by the Regents of the University of Michigan
The Museum of Anthropology
All rights reserved

ISBN (print): 978-1-949098-39-6
ISBN (ebook): 978-1-951519-63-6

Browse all of our books at
sites.lsa.umich.edu/archaeology-books.

Order our books from the University of Michigan
Press at www.press.umich.edu.

For permissions, questions, or manuscript queries,
contact Museum publications by email at umma-pubs@umich.edu or visit the Museum website at
lsa.umich.edu/ummaa.

CONTENTS

	Page
Introduction	1
Acknowledgments	4
Material	4
Separate Neural Arches	5
Herniated Vertebral Discs	14
General Anatomy	18
Detailed Lumbar Anatomy	20
Fractures of the Spine	25
Anthropometric Data	27
Discussion	35
Summary	38
Literature Cited	40

LUMBAR BREAKDOWN CAUSED BY ERECT POSTURE IN MAN[1]

INTRODUCTION

It has long been assumed that man suffers many disorders as a result of his erect posture and that bipedal locomotion imposed on an anatomy of quadrupedal heritage has caused breakdowns. The purpose in this paper is to investigate this assumption and to place in an evolutionary setting certain clinical and anatomical findings related specifically to lumbar breakdown.

Becoming erect on the ground was a critical stage in human evolution and a prerequisite to the final stages in human cerebral evolution (Weidenreich, 1941). Gross as well as minute anatomical changes were required to meet the new postural adaptation. Changes in the anatomy have resulted as new functions were imposed on old parts. Although the semierect posture of the brachiating apes would seem to have been the postural preadaptation which prepared the way for human locomotion, the addition of the lumbar curve was necessary to complete the change. This change in the anatomy of the lumbar region makes erect locomotion possible, and man alone possesses this.

Skeletally, the morphology of the lumbar region has its heritage rooted in a mammalian development adjusted to quadrupedal function. With erect posture the skeletal form remains much the same, but with considerable change in functional mechanical requirements.

In no mammal except man is there paleontological (Moodie, 1923) or modern evidence of lumbar breakdown. Nor have I seen in a search of the literature any substantial frequency of lumbar area disorders in any other mammal. It would seem, therefore, that man is unique in frequently having low back disorders.

The structural adjustment to erect posture is typically human and not limited to any one anatomical area. One such example of human locomotion adaptation is in the greater length of the lower extremities (Schultz, 1937). Many characteristics of the foot (Wood-Jones, 1916), changes in the pelvis (Darwin, 1871; Schultz, 1930), and many changes in the muscles (particularly the gluteus maximus and quadriceps extensor femoris [Hooton, 1946]) are features which clearly distinguish man from the great apes. All are concerned with upright posture.

---

[1]Submitted as partial fulfillment of the requirements for the degree of Doctor of Philosophy for the Faculty of Political Science, Columbia University.

The structural adjustment to erect posture is very old in man. Terrestial locomotion was probably the adaptation which began the separation of man from the other primates and seems to have been rapidly accomplished. In the earliest known human fossils the limb bones are essentially human although differing from modern man in details (Weidenreich, 1946, 1947). The femur of Pithecanthropus erectus was so similar to that of modern man that its correct association with the skull finds was long doubted and this morphological asymmetry gave rise to considerable discussion (Hooton, 1925). In discussing recent australopithecine finds from South Africa, LeGros Clark (1947) has this to say about these forms: "Lastly, the limb bone fragments, particularly the lower end of the humerus of Paranthropus, and the lower end of the femur of Plesianthropus, seem to indicate a limb structure which evidently approximates very closely indeed to that of Homo sapiens. This evidence of the limb bones is sufficiently startling in character to raise a doubt as to whether they actually belonged to the same creatures as the skulls of Plesianthropus and Paranthropus. That the association is entirely correct, however, seems quite well assured."

The recently announced discovery of the pelvic bones of Australopithecus prometheus (Dart, 1949) confirms the indications of upright posture seen in earlier finds. Whether these finds are considered to be in the line of evolution leading Homo sapiens is of no moment here, but they do demonstrate that the locomotive adaptation was early and not necessarily associated with other typically human morphology. This early and rapid change in posture contrasts with that in the skull, of which an almost complete series of intermediate forms is in existence, bridging the gap from earliest to recent man. The skull series is apparently so orthogenetic that some anthropologists judge the antiquity of skulls more by their situation on this morphological time scale, less with regard to their geological location. Cranial capacity, dental pattern, and many facial features exemplify the apparent gradual change.

Regions of the body as they relate to function, thus have different evolutionary patterns. The locomotor system changed from quadrupedal to bipedal very early in man's evolutionary development and has changed little since. The skull, in modifications relating to increased brain size and decrease in mastication equipment, has changed gradually and without reversals.

In contrast to the limb bones and the skull the vertebral column has changed very little in response to the demands of upright locomotion. "Man is very significantly more stable in regard to numerical variations in vertebrae than are the other forms of higher primates" (Schultz and Straus, 1945). Schultz (1930) stated that man in comparison to the anthropoids is more generalized in this region. The specialization in posture has been accomplished with little change in the vertebral column, except for the development of curves. The total effect of these evidently different rates of evolutionary reponse to the single postural change is an unbalanced adaptation. The frequency and type of structural breakdown in the spine, particularly in the lumbosacral region, seem to bear this out. In this region the anatomical adaptation to upright posture is apparently unsatisfactory and probably incomplete.

In fact the lumbar curve is probably developed anew in each individual during the growth period, and many of the typically human characteristics of the spine are similarly developed in response to function rather than inherited. The situation is similar to other skeletal features in the body which reflect upright locomotion. For example, Weidenreich (1940) has shown it to be true for the external tubercle of the tuber calcanei.

Although the lower back is particularly subject to structural disorders due to the development of the lumbar curve, other regions concerned with locomotion are also affected. Keith (1923) was the first to give a general account of the inadequacies of human adjustment to erect postural adaptations, and the matter has been gloomily reviewed by Hooton (1939). Morton (1935) traced many foot disorders back to inadequate pedal mechanics. The semilunar cartilages of the knee are frequently torn (Callander, 1939). The neck of the femur is a region of frequent fractures (Watson-Jones, 1943). In the pelvis the shortening of the lower ilium (Straus, 1927) and the development of the true bony birth canal have given rise to obstetrical difficulties (Cauldwell, Moloy, and D'Esopo, 1934). Hernia, visceral optoses, and prolapses in human beings have frequently been traced to erect posture (Keith, 1923; Gregory, 1928).

Although the idea is very old that structural weakness of the lumbosacral area followed the assumption of erect posture, the exact nature of these pathological breakdowns and their mechanics has only recently been understood. The development of orthopedic surgical techniques together with improved roentgenographic methods has made possible the diagnosis, treatment, and understanding of the mechanical breakdowns causing backache. Since 1930 voluminous clinical literature resulting from this has focused attention on conditions previously considered rare but now known to be rather common.

My purpose has been to ascertain whether or not the lumbar disorders and breakdown which plague mân are a direct result of upright posture and to investigate the mechanics of this relationship.

Two disorders were examined in detail. One is the separations in the neural arch of the vertebrae. The other is the herniations and protrusions of the intervertebral disc.

Inasmuch as anatomical lesions resulting from the mechanical strains incurred because of lumbar curvature cannot be observed in the process of their occurrence, the proof of their interrelationship must be by induction. The methodology of proof demands that the lesions be of mechanical origin, yet that their location is not due to any particular structural weakness in the area. The origin of the mechanical strains causing the lesions must next be associated with lumbar curvature. The possibility of other than lumbar mechanical strains as causes must be explored. Within these areas of proof this study was directed.

ACKNOWLEDGMENTS

I am indebted to Dr. S. L. Washburn, of the University of Chicago, for guidance in the selection of a problem and for much help in the preparation of this paper, and to Dr. H. L. Shapiro, of the American Museum of Natural History, for suggestions and help and especially for making the skeletal material of the Institute of Human Morphology available for study.

Many other persons, particularly Dr. Robert P. Ball, of the Presbyterian Hospital, New York City, and Dr. E. B. Kaplan, of the College of Physicians and Surgeons, Columbia University, have contributed considerably by their interest and by generously taking time to discuss this material with me.

The major part of this paper was prepared while I was attending Columbia University with the support of a predoctoral fellowship granted by The Viking Fund, Inc., an assistance which is here gratefully acknowledged.

MATERIAL

This paper is divided into two main sections. In Part I the location, etiology, and a discussion of the two important clinical entities receive the major attention. This is followed by a general and detailed discussion of the anatomy and mechanics of the lumbar region in relation to these two conditions. The material of Part I is largely from the literature, but includes some references to the material in Part II.

In Part II some original material related to problems discussed in Part I is presented. The data are anthropometric and are drawn from roentgenographic films of posed male medical students, from roentgenographic films of spondylolisthesis cases, and from measurements on a series of skeletons from dissection-room cadaver material. The landmarks, measurements, and methods used on this material are related to the problem of whether some particular anatomical relationship is the mechanical basis for spondylolisthesis. In addition, the mechanical relationships which appear to predispose to sacral fusion are given. This is followed by a general discussion and conclusion.

Part I

SEPARATE NEURAL ARCHES

Separations in the neural arch of the vertebrae have often been observed. Separations occurring in the neural arch at the interarticular position are known as spondylolysis and are a prerequisite for ventralward slipping of the vertebrae out of the line of the column. If slipping occurs the condition is known as spondylolisthesis.

Willis (1941) stated that "interruptions in the neural arch have been reported in all races of mankind, but not to the author's knowledge in human foetuses, or in the spinal column of any other vertebrate. This anomaly is, therefore, believed to be a consequence of upright posture." Moodie (1923) mentioned no cases in his examination of paleontological specimens. I found no cases recorded for vertebrates other than man, and it seems certain that if separations do occur they are very much less frequent than in man.

Separate neural arches are a break in the bony continuity of the spine. The security of one vertebral body to the next above and below is by way of the chain of articular facets. A lesion between any set of superior and inferior facets breaks this chain and removes the bone from the bone-muscle-ligament complex that maintains spinal stability. It must be remembered that many cases of separate neural arches occur without slipping. The age distribution of slipping in cases of spondylolysis indicates that it is probably correlated with age. So in assessing the clinical frequencies which follow, it should be remembered that separations or spondylolysis, as a prerequisite for slipping are more common than slipped vertebrae, or spondylolisthesis.

The data on the frequency and location of separate neural arches come from two general sources. One is from descriptions of prepared or archaeological skeletal series and the other from clinical series. The clinical data are less reliable in certain aspects. In the first place, not all cases of separation are found since roentgenographic technique makes the diagnosis of separations uncertain if no slipping has occurred. In the second, only selected persons come under clinical scrutiny. Usually only those suffering from low back pain are examined in the area and in sufficient detail to disclose spondylolisthesis. Some large X-ray series, however, of clinically unselected patients have been reviewed and skeletal anomalies noted. These frequencies are also included here.

There is considerable disagreement over the etiology of separate neural arches, and the frequency of its occurrence in populations varies considerably, but there is no disagreement that in pattern it is predominantly a lower lumbar region phenomenon.

History. Separated neural arches as a skeletal anomaly have been known at least since 1853 and these lesions have probably existed since man developed the lumbar curvature. Egyptian skeletal material of unstated antiquity has shown the condition (Manners-Smith, 1909). American Indian (Congdon, 1932), Eskimo (Stewart, 1931), and Lapp (Schreiner, 1931, 1935) archaeological material has instances. Owing to the rarity of remains of intact vertebral columns of early man the origin of this condition in time is unknown.

The period since 1850 has seen the recognition of separate arches as a skeletal anomaly of considerable frequency. Friberg (1939) and others credit H. F. Kilian with originating the term "spondylolisthesis" in 1853. Schwegel (1859) reported 4 cases of separations in a series of 100 European skeletal specimens.

In 47 cases that he collected up to 1882, Neugebauer (in Williams, 1899) found 53 separations (42 at L-5; 10 at L-4; 1 in the first sacral). By 1893 Neugebauer (1892) had collected 115 cases from European museum specimens and from clinical reports; of these only 7 were for males. Williams (1899) obtained 8 more cases and gave a complete review of the literature up to that time.

These authors, however, did not include Schwegel's series.

Because of the nature of the work previous to Willis (1923), no estimate of the frequency of the occurrence of this condition in any population was known. Since Willis (1923) the frequency, except in Stewart's (1931) atypical Eskimo material and in the series of Schreiner (1931, 1935), has ranged roughly around 5 per cent for many unselected series. Stewart (1931), in reporting his series, gave a review of the material reported up to that date. Since this summary little has been added except one series by Congdon (1932). I make a small addition here and give a summary of one report (Schreiner, 1931, 1935) not previously mentioned in the American literature.

With the establishment by Willis (1923, 1932) of the frequency of separate arches in a large modern American White and Negro series, clinical interest in this condition sharpened. Since then the belief that this condition caused backache, together with improvements in roentgenographic techniques, has brought hundreds of cases into the literature. Friberg (1939) stated that up to 1927 there was only a single acceptable radiologically demonstrated case of spondylolisthesis. Until 1927 the clinician was no better off in diagnosing the condition in the living than he had been in the nineteenth century.

Frequency and Location. Table I gives the frequency of separate neural arches in several series of skeletal material. Many smaller series and many tabulations which combine data from clinical and skeletal cases are not included because of lack of comparability, but most of the cases given in the literature are included.

The literature on spondylolisthesis is voluminous and reports of many cases are given without specific statement of the population from which they were derived, or exact location of the lesion in the spine, except saying that it is lumbar. The reports of Stewart (1931), Willis (reported by Stewart, 1931), Meyerding (1938), and Caldwell (1944) are given in Table II to show the vertebra location in 874 cases of both spondylolysis and spondylolisthesis.

From clinical surveys, mostly of patients who had complained of backache or some lower abdominal disturbance and had been examined with roentgenographic technique, some additional frequencies of separate neural arches have come into the literature. For the most part these findings only involve spondylolisthesis because the diagnosis of a separate arch without slipping is uncertain and difficult. Kimberly (1937) recorded 47 cases of

TABLE I

Frequency of Separations in the Neural Arch (Spondylolysis)*

Author	Date	Cases	Separate Arch	Per cent	Sex M	Sex F	Remarks - Material
Schwegel	1859	100	4	4.0	...	...	European
Turner	1886	30	4	13.3	...	...	Malay, Bushman, Esquimaux, and Negro
Hasebe	1913	125	9	7.2	84	41	Japanese
Taguchi (in Hasebe)		97	10	10.3	...	...	Japanese
Adachi (in Hasebe)		65	7	10.8	...	...	Japanese
Shore	1930	82	5	6.1	...	...	Bantu
Hayek	1928	200	6	3.0	...	...	European
Stewart	1931	348	95	27.4	182	166	Eskimo (Alaska)
Congdon	1932	200	10	5.0	...	...	American Indian (Columbia River archaeological Sites)
Willis	1932	1520	79	5.19	890	133	United States White
					400	97	United States Negro
Schreiner	1931, 1935	296	38	12.8	...	...	Lapp Archaeological Sites. 11th to 18th Century Origins.
Lanier	1939	200	12	6.0	100	...	United States White
					100	...	United States Negro
Thieme†	1948	88	3	3.4	84	4	United States Negro, White, and Oriental
Totals		3351	282	8.4			

*If the series of Stewart and Schreiner are excluded from the above tabulation, the frequency of separate arches for the remaining is 5.5 per cent. This probably is about the mean frequency for most groups.

†From a series of cadaver material. Seventy-two cases of known age, race, and sex. As follows:

	Males	Females
White.........	53	3
Negro.........	9	1
Orientals.......	6	0 (2 Japanese)
Totals.......	68	4

Average age—61.4 years.

One Japanese and two whites had separate arches at L-5. This series is from the material of The Viking Fund sponsored Institute of Human Morphology housed at the American Museum of Natural History and made available to the author by Dr. H. L. Shapiro.

TABLE II

Lumbar Location of Separate Neural Arches in Spondylolysis and Spondylolisthesis

Locations: Number and Percentage

Author	Cases	L-1 N	L-1 %	L-2 N	L-2 %	L-3 N	L-3 %	L-4 N	L-4 %	L-5 N	L-5 %	L-6 N	L-6 %	Unknown* N	Unknown* %
Stewart 1931	152	4	2.6	1	0.7	11	7.3	42	27.6	94	61.8	...	...	...	...
Willis†															
White	66	...	...	...	...	2	3.0	4	6.1	52	78.8	8	12.1	...	...
Negro	14	1	7.1	...	...	...	...	...	...	13	92.9	...	...	...	...
Meyerding 1938	583	...	...	2	0.3	3	0.5	66	11.3	480	82.4	1	0.2	31	5.3
Caldwell 1944	59	...	...	...	...	...	...	5	8.5	53	89.8	...	...	1	1.7
Totals	874	5	0.6	3	0.3	16	1.8	117	13.4	692	79.2	9	1.0	32	3.7

*"Unknown" does not mean that these cases are out of the lumbar region but is merely a result of Meyerding's system of classification. He was interested in degree of slipping in spondylolisthesis. These cases, classified as "double" or "reverse" by Meyerding, may well be in any but probably are the last or next to last segments. If L-5 and L-6 in the above chart are combined the "last lumbar segment" frequency is 80.2 per cent.
†Willis data is from Stewart, 1931.

slipping in 1157 consecutive new patients entering the clinic for low back and sciatic pain, a frequency of 4.1 per cent. Kuhns (1941) reported only 3 cases in 323 patients examined for the same complaints. Hodges and Peck (1937) found 8.1 per cent of spondylolysis or spondylolisthesis in 447 patients suffering from sciatic radiations. In this series they found that the pain patients compared to a normal control group had narrow lumbosacral disc space in the ratio of 4.5 to 1, and lumbosacral anomalies in the ratio of 2 to 1. Williams (1937) found 13 (3.25 per cent) of 400 unidentified cases had spondylolisthesis. George (1939) reported 115 cases with separate arches (108 with spondylolisthesis) in a series of 3,301 patients examined, a percentage of 3.5 per cent. Of 931 symptomless railroad employees examined routinely, reported on by Cushway and Maier (1929), and others, only 3 cases of spondylolisthesis were discovered (0.32 per cent). The doubtfulness of roentgenographic or other diagnostic techniques makes clinical-cases frequencies of less reliability than those previously listed (Table I), in which little doubt is possible in well-preserved skeletal material.

The sex distribution (Delavallade, 1932, Azema, 1932, Friberg, 1939, Meyerding, 1941) is very close to 2 to 1 for men to women. The men engaged in hard labor are more often affected than others (Meyerding, 1941).

A frequency of separate arches of 27.4 per cent was found by Stewart (1931) in a total of 350 Eskimos; of these, 187 which were from sites north of the Yukon had 39 per cent, an exceptional amount compared with other series reported (see Table I). The data of Schreiner (1931, 1935) are of interest in connection with

TABLE III

Site	No.	Cases	Per cent	Dating
Kautokeino	32	5	15.6	18th Century
Karasjok	23	8	34.8	18th Century
Auesnes	53	6	11.3	1719-1747
Kistrand	91	12	13.2	Mostly 17th, but partly 18th Century.
Neiden	62	4	6.5	18th Century
Pasvik	24	2	8.3	18th Century
Versch. Fundo	11	1	9.1	11th-12th Century
	296	38	12.8	

this. In early Lapp archaeological specimens he found the percentages for various dated sites. (See Table III, page 10)

The data in Table III seem never to have been reported before in the American literature; because of their similarity to Stewart's material both in atypically high frequency and ecological location, they are listed in detail here.

The fact that no definite evidence has been found supporting an inheritance pattern for this anomaly, and considerable against it, makes such an explanation for these two isolated high group frequencies unsatisfactory. That they are both from northern hunting and gathering primitive groups following the same generally similar life pattern due to ecological similarity is noteworthy.

Etiology of Separate Neural Arches. A discussion of the theories of the etiology of this condition is important, particularly if erect posture and lumbar curvature are basic causes. The explanation of this condition also must satisfactorily explain an incidence of approximately 5 per cent in European-American populations.

In general, if we are discussing a phenomenon in bone development the anomalous separation can only occur during three arbitrary periods of development, namely: (1) when the osteogenetic centers are laid down; (2) during development to final fusion; or as the result of (3) postfusion breaks.

Whether the condition is congenital, or not, is irrelevant because birth is not an event in bone development.

Before proceeding further, a short statement of the condition usually found at the separation point is important. Normal attempts to form repair bone callus at the lesion are lacking in all reported cases. In normal adult bone the laminae, particularly the interarticular area, is formed of very strong compact bone and very rarely fractured even in extreme trauma. The contact areas at the separation may match quite closely but no suture-like interdigitation occurs. The condition is often unilateral and so if fracture through a normal bone had occurred the intact side would hold the fracture immobile and in contact for healing. No normal repair callus repairing the break has been found. So it is extremely unlikely for it to be a phenomenon originating in period No. 3.

The age factor is important here. In the skeletal material, however, the ages are seldom known. I know of no cases of spondylolysis reported in any except adult skeletal material. Not so with spondylolisthesis. Schmorl (1932) reported 2 cases, one at 2 years and another at 2 1/2 years. Friberg (1939), in discussing the age factor, wrote that he found a case at 10 months and that Kleinberg had found one at 17 months. Cases in children and adolescents up to the end of the growth period are numerous. Infant cases are rarely reported, but this may well be due not to their absence but to lack of search for this condition which is not painful or clinically noted during childhood. The origin is probably during or previous to period No. 2.

This leads to the osteogentic period (No. 1), when the ossification centers appear in the lateral cartilage of the vertebra. If spondylolysis is to be explained as arising in this period, 2 centers of ossification must be postulated which subsequently fail to unite. There is no evidence in the literature of embryology or on separate arches which can truly support the double center theory. Rambaud and Renault (1864) described and illustrated such double centers. Hitchcock (1940), however, in speaking of this said:

> The multiplicity of ossific centers for all parts of the skeleton which these earlier observers described has never been confirmed, and it is now recognized that their erroneous observations were the outcome of artifacts created by the imperfections of the methods used in the preparation of the material. . . . Discarding the theory of multiple centers of Renault and Rambaud, a number of textbooks by authors such as Cunningham, Morris, and Keibal and Mall state that occasionally each lateral half of the 5th lumbar vertebra may ossify from two centers. Willis (1923, 1931) has indicated on what shaky foundations this assertion rests. It would seem to have been deduced from the finding of specimens showing separation of the neural arch, for no definite observations of the appearance of such double centers in foetal life have yet been reported.

Mall (1896) examined 60 embryos less than 100 days old and found no double centers. Bardeen (1905) observed: "I have, however, not found two primary ossification centers, such as Renault and Rambaud have described, for each neural arch." Chandler (1931) found none in 19 prenatal specimens. Batts (1939) concluded after examining 200, 3 to 9 months old specimens, and finding no double centers of ossification, that "whatever may be the etiology of spondylolisthesis, it is probably not on the basis of a congenital defect."

Hitchcock (1940) examined 90 more fetal specimens and found no double centers. The fact that there were no double centers in 4 series totalling 369 fetal specimens, all of which were expressly examined for this condition, makes this explanation for the 5 per cent of spondylolysis in the adult population next to impossible.

In terms of time the onset of spondylolysis begins not before birth but at infancy or early childhood, or early in period No. 2. It is very important that the development of the lumbar curve and erect posture comes at just this period. The curve develops when the child begins to walk. Mechanical-anatomical strains in this region as a result of lumbar curvature well account for separations.

Hitchcock (1940) performed experiments on a series of stillborn children and infant cadavers. In hyperflexion he was easily able to break the arch either unilaterally or bilaterally in the interarticular area and ascribed this to an hourglass shape in the ossification center with the break coming in the isthmus of the low lumbar segments. In hyperextension the anterior longitudinal ligament breaks before the arch. This demonstrates that the arch is easily broken at this time without exaggerated forces or trauma necessary to accomplish it, and also that the mechanical stresses of the area, and not necessarily localized trauma, can cause the breaks. It leaves open, however, the question of lack of repair. Possibly these breaks are quite frequent and more often healed than is known with only the nonhealing cases remaining as spondylolysis; or, possibly, blood supply or osteogenesis are interrupted because of the hourglass-shaped center where the break occurs. The pattern for this anomaly is not typical and the explanation of why osteogenesis ceases at the lesion and repair does not take place must await detailed work on this particular area in the vertebrae.

As most of the experimental work on bone and repair of fractures has been done on long bones, observations on other bones are few. It is of importance, however, to quote from Weinmann and Sicher (1947, p. 304) their discussion on variations of healing in fractures:

> The development of sealing callus is dependent on the presence of a wide marrow space. Where this is lacking, as in flat bones, without a greater amount of spongy bone, sealing callus does not form.
>
> Fractures of the bones of the skull, especially of the vault, show retarded and reduced callus formation. Very often the fragments do not undergo bony union but remain united by dense connective tissue which connects the external periosteum with the dura mater. This persistence of fibrous uniting callus cannot be regarded as evidence of failure of functional healing, since these bony fragments are often immovably fixed by their connection with the neighboring bones.
>
> The absence of a cartilaginous phase during callus formation, which has been observed frequently, has been explained by some authors on

the basis of differences in the ontogenesis of bones. Cartilaginous callus was thought to be absent in bones which develop by membranous ossification. This is not correct. Cartilaginous callus is absent in the healing of fractures of the body of the scapula, an endochondral bone. On the other hand, cartilaginous callus has been known to develop in the healing of experimental fracture of the mandible, a membrane bone. It seems more logical to assume that the mobility of the fragments and the presence of shearing forces at the site of the fracture are responsible for the formation of cartilage and that cartilage does not form where these mechanical stimuli are absent.

If the injury causes cartilage or dense connective tissue to form in the manner suggested above by Weinmann and Sicher, and this is implemented by shearing forces, which are the primary mechanical variant introduced by lumbar curvature, then the lack of callus formation is explained, Or, injury may well be in the fibro-cartilage stage preceeding final ossification, and because of this there is never even a break in bone. Repair callus or bone would not be involved at any point in the phenomena. Needless to say, much must remain on a speculative level until experimental methods are applied to the solution of these problems.

The occurrence of spina bifida with such frequency in the first sacral segment that it is practically normal, together with the high rate of bifid arch in the last lumbar, suggest that this region suffers inhibiting osteogenetic influences. If more were known about the pattern of the sequence of ossification of the lumbar region in man in relation to the typical primate or mammalian pattern, it very well might also reflect this area inhibition. At the present time this is not known. Certainly, the new mechanics of lumbar curvature imposed on a region whose heritage is from ancestral uncurved spines may have penetrating effect even into the expression of the developmental pattern of the region.

At birth the vertebral bodies all have the same shape, whereas in adult man the thoracic bodies are quite different from that of the cervical or lumbar ones (E. Th. Nauch, quoted by Slijper, 1946). The wedge shape of the last lumbar vertebrae is undoubtedly developed as an accommodation to upright posture. The postural stresses in childhood are greater relative to structural stability of the infant osseous and cartilaginous vertebral complex than at any other period. It is the time when the safety factor is lowest.

HERNIATED INTERVERTEBRAL DISCS

Herniation of the intervertebral discs occurs with considerable

HERNIATED INTERVERTEBRAL DISCS

frequency and in a great variety of directions. It occurs most often vertically into the bodies of the vertebrae superior or inferior to it. It may occur laterally in any direction through the circular annulus fibrosus which surrounds it. For anatomical reasons the pattern of lateral herniation is mostly posterior, with approximately 50 per cent in the mid-line and 50 per cent just lateral to it. In the lower lumbar region over 95 per cent of lateral herniations are posterior (Lindblom, 1944).

These posterior herniations may be sufficient to press on the spinal cord. It is the pain resulting from this pressure which has recently focused so much medical attention on herniated intervertebral discs.

Protrusions of the disc may occur with or without causing pain or ever becoming true escaping herniations. The pattern of these protrusions, though not as often a source of pain as herniations, are caused by the same thing, but are a slighter reaction.

The mechanical explanation of intervertebral disc breakdown is quite simple. The disc is a weight-bearing structure and supports all the superincumbent weight passing down the vertebral column. Disc failure results when the internal resistance of its structure is overcome by the forces acting upon it.

History. The intervertebral disc has been the subject of considerable discussion and study since Virchow's first descriptions in 1857. Reports by Goldthwaite (1911) and Dandy (1929) of spinal involvement from herniated discs were the first to indicate this as a source of pain. The work of Schmorl and Junghanns (1932), begun in 1927 on thousands of post-mortem specimens, shows the high percentage of nucleous prolapses. Beadle (1931) reporting on Schmorl's work stated that of 3,000 spines examined in 1928, 38 per cent showed disc prolapses of various kinds, and in a series of 368, 15.2 per cent of these were posterior. Schmorl did not believe them to be an important source of pain. The report of Mixter and Barr (1934) of 19 cases was the first clinical report which suggested the importance of this pathology in relation to intractable sciatic pain.

Since 1934 a voluminous literature on herniated discs has accumulated and thousands of operations to relieve pain from nerve root pressure have been performed. Dandy alone, between 1941 and 1944, operated on 843 patients to relieve intervertebral disc pressure (Lenhard, 1947).

The frequency for the general population is not accurately known, because herniations and protrusions do occur without causing pain and only those people suffering from very serious pain are usually examined in the detail which is necessary to demonstrate herniations.

Frequency. Dandy (1941) and Keys (1945) believed these herniations to be the cause of practically all serious low back pain. Few of their fellow workers would agree to this extent, but that the condition is very common is generally agreed, particularly if nonpainful breakdown of the disc is included (Symposium, (1947). As the location of the condition in relation to lumbar mechanics is the concern of this paper, the absence of reliable population frequency data, though regrettable, is not too important. This condition, except as it leaves depressions and lesions in the spongiosa of the vertebral bodies, leaves no skeletal marks in cases which have suffered from pressure on the spinal cord. These spongiosa signs can be from other causes and disc degeneration can leave similar or masking evidence, which makes examination of skeletal material unsatisfactory to obtain herniation frequency.

True herniation of the intervertebral disc, as found in operations for the relief of spinal canal involvement, is largely a lower lumbar phenomenon. Love and Walsh (1940) report on the location of 500 cases of herniated disc discovered in operations at the Mayo Clinic. Smith, Deery, and Hagman (1944) reported on 100 cases, White and Peterson (1946) on 39 cases, Barr (1938) gave location percentage for over 100 cases (assumed to be 100 in table) and these are summarized in Table IV. Poppin (1945) reported on 400 cases with location not given and Barr and Mixter (1941) reported on 155 proved cases with 90 per cent occuring in the lumbar region. They stated the "4th and 5th [were] the favored locations."

The region of next highest frequency is the lower cervical. Bradford and Spurling (1945) stated it is between 4 and 8 per cent, and most common between the fifth and seventh cervicals.

Some indication of the frequency of herniated intervertebral discs is found in the literature. Schmorl (1932) found 15.2 per cent posterior protrusions in one series. Horwitz (1939) reported only 4 instances of unilateral herniation in 75 cadaver specimens (5.3 per cent), but found 50 posterior bulgings or protrusions of the annulus fibrosus across the whole spinal canal width, but without herniation. Fifty of his 75 cases showed locations as follows: 1 between L-2 and L-3; 9 between L-3 and L-4; 19 between L-4 and L-5; and 21 between L-5 and S-1.

Batts (1939) examined 50 spines and found posterior protrusions in 16 per cent with "strong probability" that they caused symptoms in two, or 4 per cent of the cases.

Meyerding (1941) reviewed 745 cases of spondylolisthesis, diagnosed at the Mayo Clinic from 1918 to 1939 inclusive, to compare

TABLE IV

Location and Percentage Frequency of 739 Cases of Herniated Discs*

Location		Number	Percentage
Cervical	5	5	0.6
	6	5	0.6
	7	2	0.2
Thoracic	1	0	
	2	0	
	3	1	0.1
	4	1	0.1
	5	4	0.5
	6	1	0.1
	7	0	
	8	0	
	9	0	
	10	1	0.1
	11	4	0.5
	12	0	
Lumbar	1	6	0.7
	2	10	1.2
	3	50	6.1
	4	386	46.8
	5	349	42.2
Totals		825	99.8

Area Percentage

Cervical 1.4
Thoracic 1.4
Lumbar 97.0

*Data from: Love and Walsh (1940); Smith, Derry, and Hagman (1944); White and Peterson (1946); and Barr (1938). Multiple herniations in some cases account for the difference in number between cases and totals. The location figures refer to the vertebral segment; the location frequency is for the disc inferior to this segment.

incidence of sciatic pain and suspected intervertebral disc protrusion in them. Eighty cases, or 10.7 per cent had this type of pain. From 1918 to 1937 only 2 cases were suspected of intervertebral disc pressure, but from 1937 to 1938 out of 25 cases with sciatic pain 15, or 60 per cent, were suspected of disc pressure, 6 being operated upon. He believed that herniated discs were more common with spondylolisthesis than previously believed. Lumbar instability and mobility would seem to cause the disc herniation here.

Dandy (1944) recorded increased mobility between vertebral segments separated by defective discs. He said that there is no doubt about the increased mobility of the affected joint and that this is the real source of symptoms. Not all authorities agree on this symptomatic sign however. Torsion and shearing strains are equally resisted by the disc and articular facets. If increased mobility does occur it indicates that the strict confinement of the nucleus by the semirigid surrounding material is being overcome.

Herniated discs are chiefly a lower lumbar phenomena. The mechanics of the area require the intervertebral disc to perform a mechanical role at this point, a role which is lacking higher in the spine. It is the only factor which can account for the strikingly greater incidence of this lesion in this area. The fact that the planes of the inferior and superior surfaces of L-4 to L-5 and L-5 to S-1 are not parallel contributes to the insecurity. Mobility between segments is concentrated in this region and is a measure of the effect of stresses. This indicates that the longitudinal ligaments and the annulus fibrosis accommodate to the stress. In so doing the strict confinement of the nucleus is decreased. Trauma may play a role at this stage but the predisposing area weakness is the mechanical and anatomical relationships which result from lumbar curvature.

GENERAL ANATOMY

Anatomical Basis for Lumbar Weakness.[2] In relaxed erect

---

[2] For the purpose of this article the following terms are used accordingly: <u>Shear</u>—An action or stress, resulting from applied forces, which cause or tend to cause two contiguous parts of a body to slide relatively to each other in a direction parallel to their plane of contact. <u>Strain</u>—Deformation or distortion due to stress or force. <u>Stress</u>—Mutual force or action between contiguous surfaces of bodies caused by external force, as tension, shear, etc.; the cohesive force or molecular resistance in a body opposing such action. Specifically, intensity of this force, commonly expressed in pounds per square inch. (<u>Webster's Collegiate Dictionary</u>, 5th ed., 1943.)

posture man has his legs extended and his lumbar spine curved. Understanding of the anatomy which maintains this curvature is basic to a study of lumbar weakness.

All the cervical-thoracic structure rests on the lumbar spine which is not nearly so mechanically secure as are these two regions. The lumbar region of the spine is not surrounded with muscles equally distant from the vertebral bodies as they are, and the muscles between the spinous processes have little more lever arm than the cervicals yet they must resist many times greater forces. Rectus abdominous is the only anterior longitudinal muscle controlling the amount of lumbar curvature. The oblique abdominal muscles aid considerably by compressing the gut which, acting like a liquid or gas, transmits these compression forces equally in all directions thus tending to straighten out the lumbar curve and lift the thoracic cage.

Using Slijper's (1946) analogy of the bow, with the rectus abdominus the string and the vertebral column the bow, it is easy to see how this muscle controls lumbar curvature by limiting it.

Lumbar instability is a function of lumbar curvature. If the spine were straight its anatomical structure would be more secure. The vertebral bodies are built to rest one next to the other with adjacent planes parallel. In the early (11 mm.) embryo the surfaces are very nearly parallel and there are no size or shape differences between the lumbar and sacral segments (Bardeen, 1905). The structure of the intervertebral disc is best suited to this parallel relationship.

This is demonstrated by the frequency with which marginal lipping occurs. Tension in the ligaments between the vertebrae stimulates periosteal bone formation (Shore, 1935). In the spine a vertical line from the foramen magnum to the lateral malleolus passes through the spine approximately at the junction of the cervical-thoracic and thoracic-lumbar regions. These then are neutral points with the torsion between adjacent vertebrae at a minimum. In this position these intersected vertebrae in practically all motions of the spine have their adjacent planes remaining parallel and move little in relation to each other. At these same points marginal lipping is at a minimum. This does not hold for the lumbosacral joint because the sacrum remains relatively immobile and the last lumbar moves considerably on it. Approximately one-half the motion between the thoracic and pelvic regions takes place in the lumbosacral joint (Brailsford, 1945) and marginal lipping is frequent in the lumbar region. Lipping of vertebral segments which have considerable motion in relation to their adjacent segments is very marked (Shore, in Ellis, (1940)).

Lumbar curvature when the legs are extended is a function of psoas muscle shortness and forward rotation of the pelvis by the rectus femoris group. The deep back muscles tend to increase lumbar curvature if they are in tension. A muscle can only be in tension or at rest; it cannot resist compression.

To resist this backward jackknifing of the body, the extensor muscles of the legs, mainly the gluteals and hamstrings, control pelvic rotation and the abdominal muscles attaching to the thoracic cage and pelvis resist increased lumbar curvature. This whole complex of muscles maintain erect posture, together with rotation and lateral motion.

The whole muscle complex, simplified considerably in the above description, must be in a balanced relationship if the individual is to be free of low back pain. Any posture which demands that the lumbar curvature be exaggerated and which is maintained only by constant tension in the deep back muscles, or one of the other groups, will cause pain in this area. Any muscle under constant tension will eventually cause pain. If the tension is not released the pain will persist and the degree of persistence of the pain is in relation to the time the muscle has been under tension.

DETAILED LUMBAR ANATOMY IN RELATION TO HERNIATED INTERVERTEBRAL DISCS AND SPONDYLOLISTHESIS[3]

Lumbar curvature has introduced some specifically correlated mechanical strains peculiar to this area. The most important in amount is a shear component of the normal spinal forces. This causes general instability and anterior slipping following breaks in the neural arch.

All forces resulting from gravity are passed down the bone of the spinal column. These gravity forces are the total of body weight above the pelvis plus any weight the individual may be lifting or carrying. These forces may be partly resisted by compression of the gut by the abdominal muscles. This resistance is of relatively short duration, however, and probably is insignificant when a load is carried in balance, such as in a pack sack or on the head or shoulders. Yet gut compression may be of considerable help in lifting when the weight is on the arms anterior to the

---

[3] It has been assumed that the reader is familiar with general anatomy and structure of the intervertebral disc. For a detailed description of disc structure see Coventry, Ghormley and Kernohan (1945).

body. Weakening of these muscles, a normal result of sedentary occupations, is undoubtedly a factor facilitating back strain if heavy work is only occasionally done.

Computation of Compression Forces

If we consider that the arms are lifting one hundred pounds at a position anterior to mid-abdominal, the distance from the center of gravity of the load to a vertical passing through the intervertebral disc between L-3 and L-4 may be 14 inches. (This disc space is chosen because it would practically horizontal.) The deep back muscles (multifidus spinae and erector spinae) act at a point about 2 inches behind the disc fulcrum point, which is the center of the intervertebral disc. This makes the total pressure on the surface of the vertebra body 800 pounds (100 pounds of load plus 700 pounds of muscle tension to counteract it). In addition all the trunk muscles add to the disc load. This would include the rectus abdominus as a factor, with psoas adding slightly. The lateral spine stabilizing muscles, quadratus lumborum and intertransversals, add to the disc compression because they pass over the disc involved in this computation. They act posteriorly to the disc fulcrum point. All the deep back muscles act to increase the disc pressure as they compensate the anterior muscles in achieving motion stability.

Average body weight above the disc between the third and fourth lumbar vertebrae is considered here as 50 pounds. (The entire weight of the gut is supported mainly on the pelvis.) This body weight, in lifting, will be considered as centering about 4 inches anterior to the disc involved here. The sum of these static forces is:

Disc compress from load lifted. . . . . 800 pounds

Disc compress from body weight. . . . 150 pounds*

Total. . . . 950 pounds

*Fifty pounds body weight plus 100 pound deep back muscle tension to stabilize it.

This is with the body in static equilibrium. If forces required to overcome momentum or inertia are considered, momentary totals more than doubling this figure are more than likely. For easy computation in the following force analysis on the last 2 lumbar segments 1,000 pounds will be used. It must be remembered that this is not the maximum. Under traumatic crushing or rapid motion change the totals may be staggering.

Sacral Surface Angle. The angle of the fourth and fifth lumbar segments to horizontal and the angle differential between the two is a function of lumbar curvature and its sharpness. The amount of lumbar curvature necessary and its sharpness is set by the inclination of the superior surface of the sacrum. Von Luckum (1924) in a series of 30 cadaver specimens found this sacral angle to range between $28°$ and $80°$, averaging $42.5°$.[4] I estimated the angle to have a mean of $39.87 \pm .97°$ with a standard deviation of $7.07 \pm .68°$ in 53 medical students. The angle for the superior surface of the last lumbar segment averaged $18.8°$. Mitchell (1934) found a range of $32°$ to $68°$. Fletcher (1947) from a group of 200 finds an average angle of $44°$ with a range of $19°$ to $70°$. This agrees substantially with statements in anatomical literature that this angle is usually between $40°$ and $45°$.

Force Analysis at Lower Lumbar Region. If, for a force analysis, the angle of the sacral surface is considered to be $40°$ and the L-5 superior surface angle to be $20°$, a considerable shear force is indicated. One thousand pounds concentrated at the intervertebral disc between L-3 and L-4 would be passed down the column from disc to disc and from vertebra to vertebra. As a result of curvature the lower lumbar vertebral surfaces are not parallel, so the force is not compression alone. This compression force has a shear component tending to slide the superior segment anteriorally past the next lower segment. It increases as a function of the inclination of the surfaces in relation to horizontal. If the sacral surface were vertical (angle $90°$), the entire force (1,000 pounds) would shear the last lumbar past it. At $40°$ the shear component is 643 pounds; at $20°$ it is 342 pounds. As the angle increases the shear force increases as the sine of the angle.

No new muscles or ligaments have been added in man to meet the mechanical requirements of human erect posture or lumbar curvature. This curvature in normal persons may result in a very sizable shear strain which is poorly resisted by the components of man's anatomical heritage. Any tension in the lumbar musculature increases the shear forces present even at unloaded erect posture.

---

[4] Von Luckum used the plane described by the anterior pubis and the two anterior superior iliac spines as his vertical reference line. This vertical reference plane varied about 10 degrees in both directions from vertical in the series of medical students. There was no significant correlation between amount of sacral angle and the direction of variation. This reference plane is obviously arbitrary and subject to considerable change due to relaxation and postural variation, yet no body landmarks in this region are any more stable in their spatial relationships.

Lumbar Skeletal Security. The bone continuity which prevents motion response to shear forces in the lumbar region is the neural arch as it connects to the inferior articular facets and thus through successive arches to the sacrum. In fractures of the spine this arch is seldom broken which indicates that it is a relatively strong part of the vertebral segment. To test this, the safety factor for shear was computed.

Using Koch's (1917) figures for the strength of compact bone and the shear force computed previously in this paper, the safety factor was found to be 4.2. (2,700 pounds per square centimeter shear strength, from Koch, and as the arch cross-sectional area was found by me to be very close to 1 square centimeter in a series of 25 adult males specimens, the computation is $\frac{2700}{643}$ or 4.2) This is a satisfactory safety factor.

Evans and Lissner (1948) and Evans, Lissner, and Pedersen (1948) in stress coat deformation studies on long bones reported that fracture is the result of tension strains. In the intact neural arch under shear stress there is a considerable tension moment acting on the inferior anterior surface. These same moments, however, act as compression on the vertebral body. All the forces computed here have been derived from original compression forces directed down the spine and directly onto the vertebral bodies. As the bodies are of spongy bone not covered with an inferior and superior plate of compacta as in other mammals, it is understandable that this portion of the vertebral segment is more commonly fractured rather than are the facets or connecting neural arches which are of compact bone.

Where neural arch continuity is absent, as in spondylolysis, the ligaments alone prevent the shear component of the spinal compression forces from being expressed in motion. If their integrity is overcome by shearing forces, this motion is the slipping that is essential to spondylolisthesis. It was formerly believed by some that in cases of spondylolisthesis no slipping occurred because it had never been observed. Hitchcock (1940) and others have shown it does occur. In a series of spondylolisthesis films which I saw, 2 cases were observed to have progressive slipping through time.

Disc Compression in Relation to Herniation. The shear component in the normal spine when it is resisted by the articular facets and ligaments is converted into compression on the disc. In a curved spine the center of rotation is at the articular facet. The shear force acting on the vertebral body tends to rotate the vertebra causing a compression moment of this on the next lower disc.

So between the lumbar vertebrae the disc functions in compression entirely as it does in the uncurved spine. Intervertebral discs must support the total forces transmitted to them from the segment above. This is not elastically resisted by the disc center, which is incompressible liquid (From the full-term fetus and the 77 year-old adult this center decreases from 88 to 69 per cent water, averaging 80 per cent [Eckert and Decker, 1947]), but by the elastic ligaments, annulus fibrosus, and ligamenta flava which surround it. The disc is merely the structure which distributes forces. It functions to transmit forces down the spine and allows segment mobility. As previously mentioned, this transmitted compression force may be 1,000 pounds or more on the surface of the vertebrae.

The area on the normal sacral surface for a series of 50 nonfused normal or pathological sacra observed by the author, averaged very close to 2 square inches, so the disc pressure may be 500 pounds per square inch or more. The maximum is probably much higher.

With lumbar curvature the planes of adjacent vertebrae are not parallel. Although the measurement of this angle is dependent upon posture and probably time of day as well, an estimate can be obtained. I calculated the difference to average close to $10°$ in the last disc and $5°$ in the one next above.[5]

With a 10-degree angle and 1,000 pound compression force on the disc the anterior propulsion force on the entire disc is 174 pounds. However, the semiliquid nucleus pulposus transmits force acting upon it equally in all directions as would a liquid. This means any weakness, without preference to the anterior portions in any of its containing structure, if overcome, would result in herniation. It is important to stress that the forces on the disc act according to Pascal's law, as a compressed liquid or semiliquid, otherwise the high frequency of posterior herniations in relation to anterior herniation would be difficult to understand.

The posterior surface of the vertebral body is not particularly constructed to resist internal force. The posterior longitudinal ligaments do not completely cover the surface of the posterior disc and, in addition, the disc nucleus is located closer to the posterior surface than the anterior. The lumbar vertebral bodies are not circular in cross section. The spinal canal has a posterior

---

[5]In extreme hyperextension the angle may be greatly increased. In female acrobats (Kodak medical films, mentioned in Brailsford 1934), hyperextension may be so complete that the lower surface of L-3 is at $90°$ to the surface of the sacrum, with L-4 and L-5 sharing about equally in the angle difference. This would make the angle difference between adjacent vertebrae about 30 degrees.

indentation making this surface closest to the disc center. The annulus fibrosus fills the area surrounding the nucleus and is thinnest posteriorly.

Herniation into the spongiosa of the lumbar vertebra bodies is very frequent in man (38 per cent, according to Schmorl, in Beadle, 1931). They are not in themselves benign, for they may upset spinal mechanics and cause symptoms. These herniations are unique in man. He alone among mammals has no compact bone plate covering the inferior and superior spongiosa of the vertebra body. The epiphyseal ring (randleiste), which fuses to the bodies, is a complete ring (Coventry, Ghormley, and Kernohan, 1945; Inman and Saunders, 1947), but it does not cover the spongiosa as in other mammalian vertebrae. This exposes the porous uncompact center of the body to herniations. According to Inman and Saunders, this is the osmotic surface for transmission of liquid from the highly vascular spongiosa of the vertebral body to the avascular disc which maintains disc volume. Diurnal height variations in man are explained on the basis of variations in this osmotic flow, but the maintenance of disc volumes in mammals other than man, in these terms, is not explained.

FRACTURES OF THE SPINE

It might be argued that the previously discussed pathologies of the lumbar region occur there simply because it is structurally the weakest part of the spine; also, that such conditions bear no necessary relation to the addition of mechanical strain caused by lumbar curvature. To test this, the location of fractures of vertebrae caused by trauma should indicate the relative structural strength of the various spinal regions. Table V is a graph of the localization of spinal injury from 2,006 cases in the literature (Jefferson, 1928).

Two peaks in the frequency curve, at the cervical-thoracic and at the thoracic-lumbar junctions, are not associated with the lower lumbar region. Fracture points in each of the vertebrae seldom occur at the same point at which spondylolysis separations occur. The neural arch is strong compact bone. The low back is not particularly liable to fracture and the location of traumatic separations is entirely different from those previously discussed.

H. Earle Conwell (Ellis, 1940: p. 108) who reviewed a much smaller series of 126 vertebra compression fractures without cord injury in 100 adult cases reported a different pattern. Over 70 per cent of the fractures were from T-12 to L-5 inclusive, with L-1 having the highest and L-5 next highest. Although the pattern of Jefferson's cases is approximated in Conwell's, that is the peak comes at the confluence of two types of motion, these are

TABLE V

Localization of Spinal Injuries*

Localization		Cases	Percentage
Cervical	1	50	2.5
	2	95	4.7
	3	45	2.3
	4	110	5.5
	5	205	10.1
	6	250	12.4
	7	130	6.5
Thoracic	1	45	2.2
	2	25	1.3
	3	40	2.0
	4	45	2.3
	5	40	2.0
	6	36	1.8
	7	35	1.8
	8	30	1.5
	9	50	2.5
	10	70	3.5
	11	90	4.5
	12	195	9.7
Lumbar	1	205	10.1
	2	100	5.0
	3	40	2.0
	4	40	2.0
	5	25	1.2
Totals		2006	99.4

<u>Location Total Percentage</u>

Cervical..... 44.0
Thoracic..... 35.1
Lumbar....... 20.3

*Graph of the localization of spinal injury from 2006 cases in the literature from Jefferson (1928). Note the two peaks of frequency: one cervical, the other thoraco-lumbar.

clustered heavily in the lumbar region. This type of fracture, being most often caused by hyperflexion and thus not similar to Jefferson's series, shows that the region is subject to the greatest mechanical strains under this condition. Undoubtedly, compression forces sufficient to compress the vertebral bodies would also have caused disc collapse.

Ciccone and Richman (1948), in reviewing the location of 3,000 fractures and dislocations resulting from parachute jumping, reported that "fractures are not distributed uniformly throughout the spinal column. . . . the thoraco-lumbar segment is most commonly involved, particularly the first lumbar vertebra, and there is a secondary peak in the mid-dorsal region."

For the whole series they found 10 soft tissue injuries to each fracture. These findings agree with the pattern shown in Table V.

Part II

ANTHROPOMETRIC DATA

Material. If separate neural arches are to be considered a consequence of erect posture, it must be shown that these separations are not merely the result of a deviant anatomical variation. To test this possibility I examined roentgenographic films of 55 adult male medical students, posed in relaxed erect posture with standard position and distance of the ray source. These were compared with a series of films of 30 cases of spondylolisthesis.[6] In addition, 82 skeletons of known sex (with 66 of these of known race and age) were measured for comparison.[7] Three of these had separate neural arches. Unfortunately, the clinical cases of spondylolisthesis obtainable had not been posed with any anthropometry anticipated. The pose of the patients is not known. In any event the posing is not comparable to that used for the medical students. The relationships, however, which are most diagnostic of mechanical stability were measurable when sufficiently clear in the films from each series. Some films in each series were not clear for some measures so were not used in all the determinations. Although distortion in

---

[6] The films on the medical students and films of the spondylolisthesis patients were made available to the author through the courtesy of Dr. Robert P. Ball, Department of Roentgenology, Presbyterian Hospital, New York City. By making these films available, together with viewing facilities and much helpful advice, Dr. Ball made this compilation possible.

[7] Part of the collection of The Viking Fund, American Museum of Natural History, Institute of Human Morphology.

the films limited the measurements which could be used, the results have considerable reliability. Mathematical corrections were made to compensate for the distortions, but the films still do not yield the accuracy obtainable on skeletal material.

Landmarks. The lumbo-sacral region as a weight-bearing skeletal structure was measured in relation to its mechanics. Weight passes down the spine through the vertebral bones and intervertebral discs to the sacrum. It is then transmitted by the sacroiliac arch to the acetabula and thence down through the femur. Between the superior sacral surface and the acetabulum, the pelvic brim, marked by the iliopectineal or arcuate line, is the superior edge of the bony thickening which supports this weight.

In considering only weight which is transmitted to the pelvis through the vertebrae the mechanical problem is simplified. In norma lateralis the only pelvic structure relevant to this weight support is the sacral superior surface, the thick bone between the sciatic notch, the true pelvis superior brim, and the acetabulum. The pubic arch is vital in holding the pelvis in stability but does not directly transmit weight forces. The ilium is not involved because it supports viscera and is an area of muscle attachment only.

In these measurements only landmarks which are functionally related to this mechanical weight-bearing are included. The marks which are clear on radiographic films and comparable to skeletal landmarks were chosen. The points, angles, and measurements, all from norma lateralis on the films, were taken as follows (see Diagram 1, for illustration of measurements and symbols):

(1) Most superior point on the rim of the acetabulum.

(2) The angle of a line from point No. 1 to Point A, with vertical.

(3) Distance from point No. 1 to Point A. Point A is the intersection between the projected iliopectineal line and the anterior surface, or its projection, of the sacrum. (In the films this point is usually clear and corresponds to the top of the "saddle," which lies lateral to the superior surface of the sacrum and is the functional continuation of the brim of the true pelvis. The true pelvis brim is the landmark of the functionally weight-bearing bone, and the amount that the sacrum projects above and anteriorly to this line varies considerably. Using X-ray films makes the use of this important weight-bearing landmark possible. It is not an easily defined point on skeletal material.) Point A may be either anterior of posterior to the sacral promontory.

(4) The distance from the sacral promontory to Point A on the line of the anterior sacral surface.

ANTHROPOMETRIC DATA

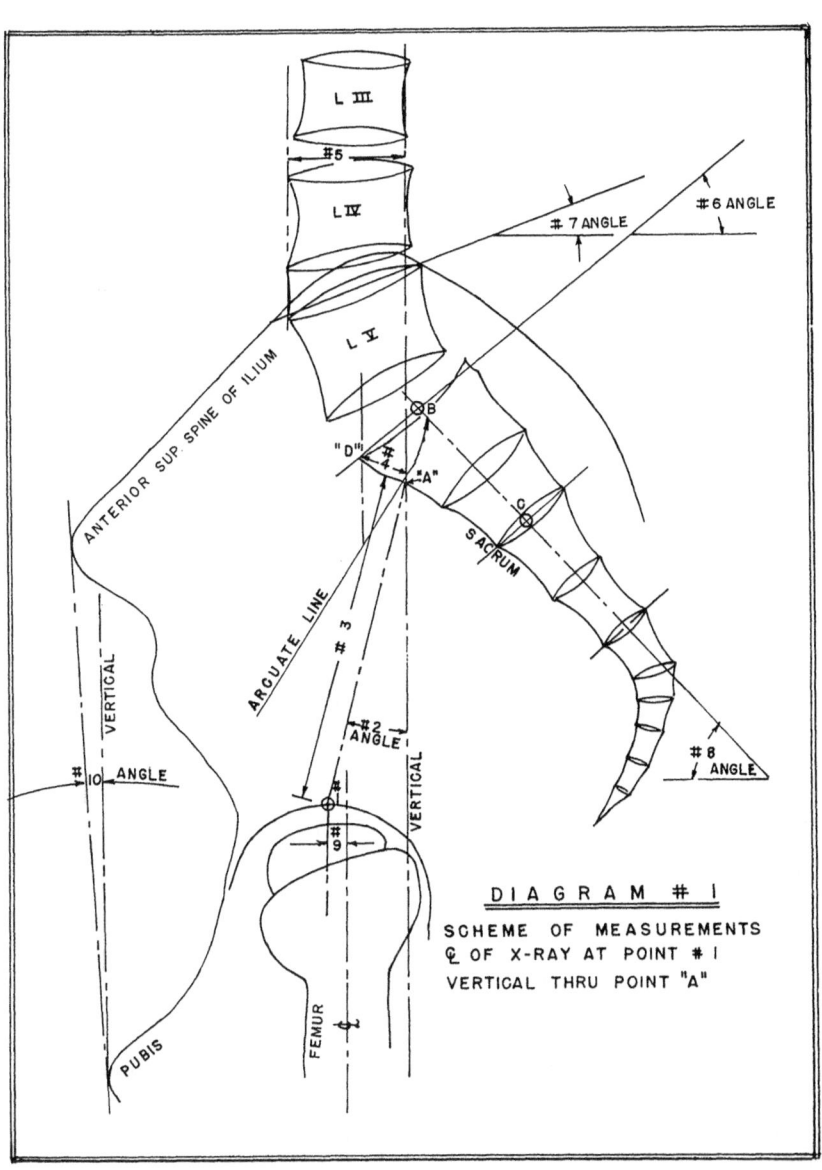

DIAGRAM # 1

SCHEME OF MEASUREMENTS
₵ OF X-RAY AT POINT # 1
VERTICAL THRU POINT "A"

(5) A measurement of lumbar curvature from a vertical passing though Point A to the point most anterior on the lumbar vertebrae.

(6) The angle of inclination of the superior articular surface of the sacrum with horizontal.

(7) The angle of inclination of the superior surface of the last lumbar vertebra with horizontal.

(8) The angle of inclination of the sacrum with horizontal. It is measured by a line drawn through points bisecting the superior surface of the first sacral segment with another bisecting the inferior surface of the second segment (Points B and C). Some authors have connected points made by drawing diagonals from the corners of these two segments or other lower segments, but this was not done here as it tends to increase the inaccuracies because sacral segment length becomes involved in relation to curvature.

(9) The distance from a vertical passing through the center line of the shaft of the femur with point No. 1.

(10) The angle of inclination to vertical of the plane described by the anterior point of symphysis pubis and the superior anterior iliac spines.

Methodology. In evaluating the data from the various sources presented here some assumptions were basic to the methodology used. It was assumed that any unusual deposition of bone or fusing of two normally separate segments indicated that this is the result of mechanical imbalance. In particular, fusing of the last lumbar segment to the sacrum or ilium, or sacralization, was assumed to be an indication of extensive marginal lipping ending in fusion. This lipping is an ossification of ligament and connective tissue under tension. The reaction of the skeleton in these cases is explained as a result of the increase of any physiologic stress in the limits of tolerance which acts as a growth stimulus on bone (Weinmann and Sicher, 1947: p. 147). It is a protective mechanism and examples of it occur throughout the body. The process of fusing may originate in trauma or through disc degeneration. If the area were not under unusual mechanical stress, the process might not in these cases continue and reach a complete fusion. This is, of course, excluding cases of pathological bone development.

In all the material observed the presence or absence of fusing, scoliosis, or any other abnormalities were noted. The hospital history of spondylolisthesis cases was noted. In general, any conditions which might be related to anatomical mechanical imbalance were considered. Much of the data and many of the measurements were discarded because of questionable accuracy or because the findings proved of no value in relation to the central problem.

Angle No. 10 was used to test von Luckum's (1924) assumption that a plane determined by the pubis and anterior superior spines of the ilium is a vertical plane of reference for use in making measurements of pelvic and sacral angles on cadaver material. In the series of posed medical students it was within plus or minus 10 degrees. This would seem to make the plane a somewhat unrealistic vertical; however, for an anatomical reference plane it is valuable because it is easily determined and no substitution is more accurate.

The central ray of the films was set to pass through the heads of the femurs from norma lateralis (aimed at the head nearest the tube). Any measurements on the film decrease in accuracy as they are distant from this center of penetration. As previously mentioned, corrections were made from this. If all the points used in measuring are not on the same sagittal plane, they cannot be reliably compared. The data used satisfy this requirement. The only exception is that the point of intersection of the arcuate line and the sacrum are not on the same plane as the sacral promontory. So in all instances the points on the film where the arcuate lines of both sides intersect the anterior inferior surface of the sacrum were marked. The point used for measurement was midway between these two points. Theoretically, this should place the point used for measurement on the sagittal plane.

Because of the accuracy limitations just mentioned, only three measures were used. The angles of sacral inclination and the superior sacral articular surface to horizontal have obvious value in the mechanical functioning of the area. In a general respect they are related and of the two the articular inclination is the more important. The one other measurement used (No. 4) was theoretically determined to be important because it involves the point (Point A) in the pelvic bone mass, where the forces transmitted down the spine are separated and pass out to the femur through the pelvic arch. It shows on the norma lateralis films because of this dense weight-carrying bone structure. This point in relation to the sacral promotory showed a highly significant relationship to lumbosacral fusion.

<u>Sacral Angle.</u> This angle (No. 8 in the diagram) was determined on the students and the spondylolisthesis cases. Because of lack of clarity in some films for this measurement only 54 students and

22 clinical cases were used. For the medical students the results, with standard errors, are as follows:

Mean .... $34.39 \pm .75^0$

Standard Deviation .... $5.48 \pm .53^0$

Number 54

Range .... 22^0 to 51^0

For the 22 cases of spondylolisthesis (12 male, 9 female, and 1 of unknown sex) only the mean was determined. It was 34.09 ± 2.02^0. Little reliability can be given to this figure, because the posing of the patients is unknown. It also is a combination for both sexes. If the figure is of any value, it may show that these cases vary but little from the posed male medical student in this respect.

Angle of Superior Sacral Articular Surface (No. 6) with standard errors.

Mean .... $39.87 \pm .97^0$
Standard Deviation .... $7.07 \pm .68^0$
Number 53
Range .... 23^0 to 54^0

Because of lack of reliability this angle is not given for the spondylolisthesis cases.

Distance from Sacral Promotory to the Intersection of the Arcuate line and the Sacrum. (Distance No. 4 in millimeters):

A. Cases without fusions it is as follows:

Sample:	Students	Spondylolisthesis	Museum Skeletons
Mean:	$19.96 \pm .34$mm.	13.04 ± 1.60mm.	$17.66 \pm .51$mm.
S.D.:	$2.38 \pm .24$mm.	8.02 ± 1.14mm.	$4.15 \pm .36$mm.
Number:	49	25	67
Range:	+5 to +39	+0 to +28	+8 to +28

B. Cases with fusions:

Sample:	Students	Spondylolisthesis	Museum Skeletons
Mean:	1.17 ± 1.77mm.		5.07 ± 2.24mm.
S.D.:	4.34 ± 1.26mm.		8.69 ± 1.59mm.
Number:	6 (11.1%)		15 (18.3%)
Range:	-7 to +6		-20 to +19

C. Cases with nonfusion and fusion compared:

    Difference: 21.13mm.   12.59mm.
    Variance Ratio (t) [8]: 11.7   5.5

When the sacral promontory is inferior and posterior to Point A (located at the intersection of the arcuate line and an extended line from the anterior sacral surface) the distance was considered to be a negative number. The fact that a zero measurement or a negative number is possible under this system of measurement does not affect the reliability of the means or standard deviation, but it makes the coefficient of variation a meaningless calculation. This coefficient is therefore omitted.

It is of interest to note that with only one exception among male medical students with fusion (6mm.) is there any case which comes within the range of distribution of the medical students without fusion. For the museum series (all male, but with a racial distribution of 9 negro [none fused], 6 oriental [1 fused], 51 white [8 fused], and 16 of unknown age and race [6 fused]), this segregation is not so clear. It is a slightly larger series and it is an older series. Average age for the medical students was 24.4 years, whereas for the museum series in cases of known age it was 61.4. The museum series (prepared from dissecting room cadavers) and the student series are obviously not one homogeneous population. Yet within each series and between both, the differences of the fused and nonfused cases is striking and highly significant.

The variance ratio (t) clearly indicates that the difference between the fused and nonfused cases in each sample is not due to chance. Some relationship certainly exists between the variations in this measurement (No. 4) and the presence or absence of fusion. This relationship is also quite clearly attributable to some mechanical factor.

Point A in these measurements is a functional point and not one arbitrarily chosen because of tradition or ease of measurement. It is related to the mechanical problem at hand and was

---

[8] The variance ratio (t), a measure of the significance of difference, is computed here by dividing the difference between the means (D) being tested by the square root of the sum of the squares of the Standard Errors of these Means.

$$\sigma_D = \sqrt{\frac{\sigma_1^2}{N_1} + \frac{\sigma_2^2}{N_2}}, \qquad t = \frac{D}{\sigma_D}$$

If the ratio value is 2, the chance is approximately 1 in 20 that the difference is due to chance. Ratio values greater than 2 make the possibility that there is a significant difference between the means more likely.

chosen for that reason. Whether it is safe to say that people who have a short No. 4 distance are predisposed to lumbosacral fusions is not known. Larger series and the application of this test to individuals through their life span can only determine this.

Yet based on a mechanical analysis it seems to be clear why this relationship exists. If the point of separation of the forces that are transmitted down the spine and out to the femur is anterior to the sacral promontory, they do not go through the sacrum. The last lumbar vertebra is also anterior to the sacrum. The sacrum, which is then out of the direct line--or partly so--of force transmission, does not perform its mechanical functions normally. New bone built up in response to these abnormal tensions bridges from the last lumbar to the sacrum or ilium to give a security that the unossified ligaments and connective tissue cannot.

In the No. 4 measurement between the nonfusion cases with and those without spondylolisthesis, there are significant statistical differences. The difference in means is 5.29 mm. between the spondylolisthesis and student series, and 4.63 mm. between spondylolisthesis and museum series. This is a significant difference. It is necessary, however, to point out here that this analysis was between fusion and nonfusion cases. If the fusion cases are recombined with the nonfusion in student and museum samples, the differences are greatly reduced and lose significance when compared with the spondylolisthesis (value of t is less than 2.).

It is difficult to imagine that differences of this magnitude can be significant in the mechanical analysis of forces which might cause spondylolisthesis, particularly when the fusion cases are so much farther in the direction of the difference yet do not show the condition.

Only the most meaningful results are presented. The following account of the several relationships which were tested are given. It was found that in general the angles Nos. 6 and 7 were inversely related with the angle No. 8 and, that as the angle No. 2 increased angle number 8 increased. This is probably all due to a rotation of the pelvis. A scatter diagram shows that there is a slight tendency for No. 4 to decrease as No. 7 increases. The functional importance of this is not apparent. Owing to the small size of the fusion samples, all of the possible relationships were not tested one to the other and to the presence of fusions. However, the possible deviations which might explain the occurrence of spondylolisthesis were examined and none found conclusive. This, after all, was the purpose of the investigation.

It is suggested from these findings that the definition of the first sacral segment might be that segment which is the first with any part anterior and superior to Point A. On mechanical grounds it may be valid to say that the first sacral segment is the last segment in the spinal column which is involved directly with the transmission of weight forces from the spine to the legs and is superior to the intersection of the plane of the arcuate lines with the sacrum.

DISCUSSION

Separate neural arches and herniated intervertebral discs are predominantly a phenomena of the lower lumbar spine. The explanation of the frequency and location of these lesions must be found within certain areas. These are discussed and summarized here.

An inheritance pattern for these conditions has been suggested. Friberg (1939) believed there to be one for spondylolysis on the evidence from one family which included 7 cases. Brailsford (1945) stated that several authors have contended that a familial pattern exists. Hitchcock (1940) suggested that birth difficulties resulting from spondylolisthesis might cause trauma which would account for this apparent pattern. Among all the etiological explanations for spondylolisthesis, summarized by Brailsford (1945), no conclusive evidence showing an inheritance pattern is given. None is postulated to explain herniated discs.

Neither condition is believed by any authority to be related to a specific pathological entity.

Aging is of importance in both conditions in that they occur mainly in the fourth decade. Spondylolisthesis has been demonstrated to occur as early as 10 months (Friberg, 1939), and though its diagnosis in middle life is largely due to the onset of pain, the time of separation has never been established certainly. Normal skeletal age changes, however, do not account for these anomalous separations.

For discs the aging factor is more important in the etiology of herniation. Inman and Saunders (1947) found that the water content of the nucleus is changed as the cartilage plate covering the vertebral bodies becomes less permeable. This decrease occurs with increasing age and results in a progressive dessication of the nucleus. Dessication changes the disc structure and in effect reduces the safety factor resisting unchanged normal stresses acting on this structure. Spondylosis deformans or marginal lipping is also an outcome of degeneration of the disc. Yet aging, as shown by the pattern of distribution, is only indirectly the cause of herniations. It predisposes the vertebral segments under greatest strain to herniations. It decreases the safety factor.

Sex has not proved to be a factor in the cause of either of these conditions even though males are affected twice as often as females, and of all males those engaged in hard labor more than others (Meyerding, 1941; Love, 1947). No evidence indicates the lesions are caused by secondary sex changes or by sexual differentiation in development. Danforth (1930) suggested that sex may be an important determinant even in the variation of vertebral count. It may be of some unknown importance in the etiology of these lesions, at least as far as sex differences in frequency are concerned.

These lesions are not associated with any conditions known to be caused by low nutrition such as osteomalacia. The localized area of their occurrence weighs against such a cause.

Stewart (1931) suggested that racial factors might account for the different frequencies for separate arches, which have been observed between populations. But, he said, there is not sufficient proof for this theory. No additional proof has been accumulated since his articles.

It is more likely, in view of the findings of Schreiner (1931,1935), together with those of Stewart (1931), that ecological conditions instead of racial factors may be more important in the case of separate arches. Both groups, studied Lapp and Eskimo, live in rigorous northern environments and show, atypically high frequencies, particularly in subsamples of their total groups. As suggested previously, this may be a fruitful area of investigation. Possibly some factor in their life patterns and activities associated with the environment causes the condition. Other high latitude groups should be investigated to see if this is borne out.

In the case of separate arches, normal developmental variations have been suggested by many authors to be the cause of this condition. This has been fully discussed in a previous section and appears to be without sufficient basis to account for the frequency found in populations. Keith (in Ellis, 1940) summarized current opinion when he stated, "I know of no evidence which leads me to suppose that the separation of the arch of the last lumbar vertebrae is the result of mal-development."

Three series of specimens were tested by me to ascertain whether spondylolisthesis could be attributed to some deviant mechanical relationship. The results were negative.

Mechanical strain has been shown to be the logical cause of these lesions. This has been done not by a process of elimination, but by the demonstration that shear forces, which are the mechanical consequence of lumbar curvature, are the active factor. These shear forces may be the result of trauma or normal strain.

The frequency distribution pattern of spinal fractures does not coincide with the pattern for either separate arches or herniated discs. This eliminates the possibility that the lesions are merely the result of strain acting on a structurally weak area.

The detailed process of the occurrence of these lesions is not known because they have never been observed. Yet it seems certain that mechanical strains overcome the resistance, or stress, of the anatomical structure causing lesions. The nature of this strain is a shearing force. This shearing force is the consequence of lumbar curvature. Lumbar curvature is a consequence of erect posture.

Erect posture was an early adaptation in man. The vertebral column has been subjected to the pressures of erect posture throughout man's evolutionary history with little effect.

The evolution of the lumbar curve is unknown. This curvature has been noted in other vertebrates, particularly in the higher primates (Cunningham, 1886), but is relatively very much less than in man. It is even extremely doubtful whether the lumbar curve is itself inherited. It only develops as the child sits up and walks. In the newborn child the vertebral bodies have altogether the same shape. In the adult man the shape of the thoracic bodies is quite different from that of the cervical or lumbar ones (E. Nauck, Th. in Slijper '46). The curve probably represents a mechanical adjustment between the human pelvis and lower extremities and an essentially anthropoid vertebral column which is worked out anew during the lifetime of each individual. The fact that the curve is developed before epiphyseal union of the neural arch occurs in the lower vertebrae is probably of great importance in the occurrence of anomalies in the region, (Callander, 1939).

It is difficult to see why the adaptation of the vertebral column has been so suppressed phylogenetically. The explanation of the apparent dysplastic anatomical adaption of the different regions of the body to the mechanical requirements of upright posture may be dictated by the amount of selective pressure involved. The rates of change of the regions were evidently different and the limits of adaptation attainable are unknown. The different rates of adjustment evidenced by the lower limbs and the spine, for example, are probably the result of ecological pressure at a very critical stage in human evolution. The terrestial adaptation was a drastic and critical one. The semierect preadaptation which made terrestrial life possible was probably quite gradual but the change to the new completely terrestrial mode and fully erect posture must have been a rapid adaptation. The limb and pelvic adjustment which made this possible was early and since then has been quite stable. In this it appears that man went through a period of rapid quantum evolution, in Simpson's (1944) terms, which allowed him to reach a new and advantageous general equilibrium unlike the ancestral condition. Terrestrial adaptation brought about the origins of a new group. Yet, the human spine, which is generally similar in motion limits and structure to the other higher primates, seems to have been quite unaffected. Having made a successful locomotion adaptation, including the lumbar curve, the functional locomotive structure of man has subsequently been stable.

This stability is no doubt made possible by the apparently slight selective pressure mitigating against the person suffering from the lesions discussed. The average age of breakdown is late, about forty (Love, 1947). This is well along in the reproductive period and rarely lethal. Often considerable degrees of slipping in spondylolisthesis occur without hindrance to childbirth, (Kaplan, 1948). It is difficult to see that selective pressure for change in the vertebral structure of man has been considerable. Yet many sections of the body have undergone considerable change apparently with no greater selective pressure. Perhaps, it is enough to say that there are uneven rates of adaption and evolution within the anatomical regions of the body, just as there are between closely related species.

SUMMARY

1. The assumption that disorders and breakdown occur in the low back because of erect posture in man was tested in this study in the light of recent knowledge about the frequency, location, and mechanics of two clinical entities. These are separate neural arches, with or without spondylolisthesis, and herniated intervertebral discs. These conditions were investigated in detail to see if their occurrence can be associated with erect posture, or more specifically, with lumbar curvature.

2. The frequency of separate neural arches in a summary of many series, totalling 3351 cases, was 8.4 per cent. The location of the condition in the spine, together with spondylolisthesis, in 874 cases was found to be a lumbar phenomenon. Within the lumbar region, 80.2 per cent were at the last lumbar vertebra, and 97.3 per cent were in the last two vertebral segments.

3. The locations of 825 cases of intervertebral disc herniations are given, 97.0 per cent of these were in the lumbar region and 89.0 per cent were in the last two vertebral discs.

SUMMARY

4. The mechanics of lumbar curvature was investigated to test the frequency and location of the two clinical conditions, as well as their etiology, in terms of a mechanical explanation.

5. The location of over 2,006 spinal fractures was given to demonstrate that the location and frequency of separate neural arches and intervertebral disc herniations are not due to localized structural weakness in the lower lumbar region.

6. Original material includes anthropometric measurements from roentgenographic films of 55 male medical students and 30 cases of spondylolisthesis, together with measurements from a skeletal series of 82, which were made to test whether the location and etiology of spondylolisthesis is merely the result of some deviant anatomical relationship and not of lumbar curvature. This proved negative. From this material it developed, however, that one deviant anatomical relationship apparently predisposes to the natural fusion of the last lumbar segment to the sacrum. From this a new method of defining the first sacral segment is proposed.

7. In conclusion, it was found that the mechanical strains resulting from erect posture and lumbar curvature, particularly a shear component of the vertical compression forces, are the contributory cause of the two types (spondylolisthesis and herniated intervertebral discs) of low back breakdown which are discussed here.

8. A short discussion of the evolutionary adaptations of man, in relation to the assumption of erect posture, is included.

LITERATURE CITED

Azema, M. A. Le Spondylolisthesis. Paris: Jouve & Cie, 1932.
Bardeen, C. R. Studies of the Development of the Human Skeleton. Amer. Journ. Anat., 4 (1905): 265.
Barr, J. S. Intervertebral Disk Lesions as Cause of Sciatica. Brit. Med. Journ., 1247 (1938).
Barr, J. S., and W. J. Mixter. Posterior Protrusions of the Lumbar Intervertebral Disc. Journ. Bone Joint Surg., 23 (1941): 444.
Batts, Martin, Jr. Rupture of the Nucleus Pulposus. Journ. Bone Joint Surg., 21 (1939): 121.
Batts, Martin, Jr. The Etiology of Spondylolisthesis. Journ. Bone Joint Surg., 21 (1939): 879.
Beadle, Ormand A. The Intervertebral Discs. Observations on Their Normal Anatomy in Relation to Certain Spinal Deformities. Med. Res. Council, Special Rept. Ser., No. 161. London: His Majesty's Stationery Office, 1931.
Bradford, F. K., and R. G. Spurling. The Intervertebral Disc. 2d.; Springfield, Ill. 2: Charles C. Thomas, 1945.
Brailsford, J. F. The Radiology of Bones and Joints. Baltimore: W. Wood and Co., 1934 and 1945.
Caldwell, G. A. Spondylolisthesis. Analysis of Fifty Nine Cases. Ann. Surg., 119 (1944): 485.
Callander, C. L.: Surgical Anatomy. 3d ed. 3; Philadelphia: W. B. Saunders Co., 1939.
Cauldwell, W. E., H. C. Moloy, and D. A. D'Esopo. Further Studies in the Pelvic Architecture. Amer. Journ. Obstet. Gynecol., 28 (1934): 482.
Chandler, F. A. Lesions of the "Isthmus" (Pars Interarticularis) of the Laminae of the Lower Lumbar Vertebrae and Their Relation to Spondylolisthesis: Surg. Gynecol. Obstet., LIII (1931): 273.
Ciccone, Roy, and R. M. Richman. The Mechanism of Injury and the Distribution of 3000 Fractures and Dislocations Caused by Parachute Jumping. Journ. Bone Joint Surg., 30A (1948): 77.
Clark, W. E. LeGros. Observations on the Anatomy of the Fossil Australopithecinae. Journ. Anat., 81: (1947): 300.
Congdon, Russel T. Spondylolisthesis and Vertebral Anomalies in Skeletons of American Aborigines. Journ. Bone Joint Surg., 14 (1932): 511.
Coventry, M. B., R. K. Ghormley, and J. W. Kernohan. The Intervertebral Disc. Pts. I, II, III. Journ. Bone Joint Surg., 27 (1945): 105, 233, 460.
Cunningham, D. J. The Lumbar Curve in Man and the Apes. Royal Irish Acad., Cunningham Mem., No. 2, 1886.
Cushway, B. C., and R. J. Maier. Routine Examination of the Spine for Industrial Employees. Journ. Amer. Med. Assn., 92 (1929): 701.
Dandy, W. E. Loose Cartilage from the Intervertebral Disk Simulating Tumor of the Spinal Cord. Arch. Surg., 19 (1929): 660.

LITERATURE CITED

Dandy, W. E. Concealed Ruptured Intervertebral Disks. A plea for the Elimination of Contrast Mediums in Diagnosis. Journ. Amer. Med. Assn., 117 (1941): 821.

Dandy, W. E. Treatment of Recurring Attacks of Low Backache without Sciatica. Journ. Amer. Med. Assn., 125 (1944): 125.

Danforth, C. H. Numerical Variations and Homologies in Vertebrae. Amer. Journ. Phys. Anthropol. 14 (1930): 463.

Dart, R. A. The First Pelvic Bones of Australopithecus prometheus: Preliminary Note. Amer. Journ. Phys. Anthropol., N. S., 7 (1949): 225.

Darwin, Charles. The Descent of Man and Selection in Relation to Sex. New York: D. Appleton & Co., 1871.

Delavallade, P. P. A. Contribution a l'etude de Spondylolisthesis. Bordeaux: These, 1932.

Eckert, C., and A. Decker. Pathological Studies of Intervertebral Discs. Journ. Bone Joint Surg., 29 (1947): 447.

Ellis, J. D. The Injured Back and its Treatment. Springfield, Ill.: C. C. Thomas and Co., 1940.

Evans, F. G., and H. R. Lissner. "Stresscoat" Deformation Studies of the Femur under Static Vertical Loading: Anat. Rec., 100 (1948): 159.

Evans, F. G., H. R. Lissner, and H. E. Pedersen. Deformation Studies of the Femur under Dynamic Vertical Loading. Anat. Rec. 101 (1948): 225.

Fletcher, G. H. Backward Displacement of the Fifth Lumbar Vertebrae in Degenerative Disc Disease. Journ. Bone Joint Surg., 29 (1947): 1019.

Friberg, Sten. Studies on Spondylolisthesis. Acta Chirurg. Scand.,82, Suppl. 55 (1939).

George, E. M. Spondylolisthesis. Surg. Gynecol. Obstet., 68 (1939): 774.

Goldthwaite, J. E. The Lumbo-Sacral Articulation; An explanation of many cases of 'Lumbago', 'Sciatica' and 'Paraplegia'. Boston Med. Surg. Journ., 164 (1911): 365.

Gregory, W. K. The Upright Posture of Man; A Review of its Origin and Evolution. Proc. Amer. Philos. Soc., LXVII, No. 4 (1928).

Hasebe, K. Die Wirbelsaule der Japaner. Z. Morph. u. Anthrop., XV (1912-13): 259.

Hayek, H. Über Spondylolysis. Zentralbl. f. Gynak., LII (1928): 2511.

Hitchcock, H. H. Spondylolisthesis; Observations on its Development, Progression, and Genesis. Journ. Bone Joint Surg., 22 (1940): 1.

Hodges, F. J., and W. S. Peck. Clinical and Roentgenological Study of Low Back Pain with Sciatic Radiations. Amer. Journ. Roentgenol., 37 (1937): 461.

Hooton, E. A. The Assymetrical Character of Human Evolution. Amer. Journ. Phys. Anthropol. 8 (1925): 125.

Hooton, E. A. Twilight of Man. New York: G. P. Putnam's Sons, 1939.

Hooton, E. A. Up from the Ape. Rev. ed.; New York: Macmillan, 1946.

Horwitz, Thomas. Lesions of the Intervertebral Disk and Ligamentum Flavum of the Lumbar Vertebrae; an anatomic study of 75 human cadavers. Surgery 6 (1939): 410.

Inman, V. T., and J. B. de C. M. Saunders. Anatomicrophysiological Aspects of Injuries to the Intervertebral Disc. Journ. Bone Joint Surg., 29 (1947): 461.

Jefferson, G. Discussion of Spinal Injuries. Proc. Roy. Soc. Med., 21 (1928): 21.

Kaplan, E. B. Personal Communication, 1948.

Keith, Sir A. Man's Posture; Its Evolution and Disorders. Brit. Med. Journ., 1 (1923): 451, 499, 545, 587, 624, 669.

Keys, J. A. Intervertebral Disk Lesions are the Most Common Cause of Low Back Pain with or without Sciatica. Ann. Surg., 121 (1945): 534.

Kimberley, A. G. Low Back Pain and Sciatica; Its Etiology, Diagnosis and Treatment. Surg. Gynecol. Obstet., 65 (1937): 195.

Koch, John C. Laws of Bone Architecture. Amer. Journ. Anat., 21 (1917): 177.

Kuhns, John G. Conservative Treatment of Sciatic Pain in Low Back Disability. Journ. Bone Joint Surg., 23 (1941): 435.

Lanier, R. R., Jr. The Presacral Vertebrae of White and Negro Males. Amer. Journ. Phys. Anthropol., 25 (1939): 341.

Lenhard, R. E. End-Result Study of the Intervertebral Disc. Journ. Bone Joint Surg., 29 (1947): 425.

Lindblom, K. Protrusion of Disks and Nerve Compression in the Lumbar Region. Acta Radiologica, 25 (1944): No. 145.

Love, J. G. The Disc Factor in Low-Back Pain, with or without Sciatica. Journ. Bone Joint Surg., 29 (1947): 438.

Love, J. G., and M. N. Walsh. Intraspinal Protrusion of Intervertebral Disks: Arch. Surg., 40: (1940): 454.

Luckum, von H. L. The Lumbo-sacral Region; an Anatomical Study and Some Clinical Observations. Journ. Amer. Med. Assn., 82 (1924): 1109.

Mall, F. P. On Centers of Ossification in Human Embryos Less Than 100 Days Old. Amer. Journ. Anat., 5 (1896): 433.

Manners-Smith, T. The Variability of the Last Lumbar Vertebrae. Journ. Anat., XLIII (1909): 146.

Meyerding, H. W. Spondylolisthesis as an Etiologic Factor in Backache. Journ. Amer. Med. Assn., 111 (1938): 1972.

Meyerding, H. W. Low Backache and Sciatic Pain Associated with Spondylolisthesis and Protruded Intervertebral Disc; Incidence, Significance, and Treatment. Journ. Bone Joint Assn., 23 (1941): 461.

Mitchell, G. A. G. The Lumbosacral Junction. Journ. Bone Joint Assn., 16 (1934): 233.

Mixter, W. J., and J. S. Barr. Rupture of the Intervertebral Disc with Involvement of the Spinal Canal. New Eng. Journ. Med., 211 (1934): 210.

Moodie, R. L. Paleopathology. Urbana, Ill.: Univ. Ill. Press, 1923.

Morton, D. J. The Human Foot. New York, 1935.

Murray, P. D. F. Bones; A Study of the Development and Structure of the Vertebrate Skeleton. Cambridge: Cambridge Univ. Press., 1936.

Neugebauer, F. Spondylolisthesis et Spondylizeme. Paris, 1892.

LITERATURE CITED

Poppen, James L. The Herniated Intervertebral Disk; An Analysis of 400 Verified Cases. New Eng. Journ. Med., 232 (1945): 211.

Rambaud, A., and Ch. Renault. Origine et developpement des os. Paris, 1864.

Schmorl, George: Beitrag zur Kenntnis der Spondylolisthese. Deutche Zeitschr. f. Chir., 237, (1932). Hft. 7, 8, 9; 422.

Schmorl, G., und H. Junghanns. Die gesunde und kranke Wirbelsaule in Roentgenbild. Leipzig: Georg Thieme, 1932.

Schreiner, K. E. Zur Osteologie der Lappen. Instit. f. Sammenlignende Kulturforsk. Series B: Skrifter Vol. 18-1, Oslo, 1935; Vol. 18-2, Oslo, 1931.

Schultz, A. H. The Skeleton of the Trunk and Limbs of Higher Primates. Human Biol., 2 (1930): 303.

Schultz, A. H. Proportions, Variability and Asymmetries of the Long Bones of the Limbs and the Clavicles in Man and Apes. Human Biol. 9 (1937): 281.

Schultz, A. H., and W. L. Straus. The Numbers of Vertebrae in Primates. Proc. Amer. Philos. Soc., 89 (1945): 601.

Schwegel, Andr. Knochenvarietaten. Zeitschr. f. rat. Med., 283 (1859).

Shore, L. R. Abnormalities of the Vertebral Column in a Series of Skeletons of Bantu Natives of South Africa. Journ. Anat., 64 (1930): 206.

Shore, L. R. Polyspondylitis marginalis osteophytica. Brit. Journ. Surg., 22 (1935): 850.

Simpson, G. G. Tempo and Mode in Evolution. New York: Columbia Univ. Press, 1944.

Slijper, E. J. Comparative Biologic-Anatomical Investigations on the Vertebral Column and Spinal Musculature of Mammals. Kon. Ned. Akad. We., Verh. (Tweede Dectie), Dl. XLII, No. 5, 1946.

Smith, A. de F, E. M. Deery, and G. L. Hagman. Herniation of the Nucleus Pulposus. A Study of 100 Cases Treated by Operation. Journ. Bone Joint Surg., 26 (1944): 821.

Stewart, T. D. Incidence of Separate Neural Arch in the Lumbar Vertebrae of Eskimos. Amer. Journ. Phys. Anthropol., 16 (1931): 51.

Straus, W. L. The Human Ilium; Sex and Stock. Amer. Journ. Phys. Anthropol., 11 (1927): 1.

Symposium on Intervertebral Disc. Journ. Bone Joint Surg., 29 (1947): 424.

Turner, Sir Wm. Report on the Human Crania and other Bones of the Skeletons Collected During the Voyage of H. M. S. Challanger, in the Years 1873-76. 2d Pt, Zoology, Vol. 16. 1886. Printed for Her Majesty's Stationery Office.

Watson-Jones, R. Fractures and Joint Injuries. 2d ed., Edinburgh: Livingstone, 1943.

Weidenreich, F. The External Tubercle of the Human Tuber Calcanei. Amer. Journ. Phys. Anthropol., 26 (1940): 473.

Weidenreich, F. The Brain and its Role in the Phylogenetic Transformation of the Human Skull. Trans. Amer. Philos. Soc. (N.S.), 31 (1941): 321.

Weidenreich, F. Apes Giants and Man. Chicago: Univ. Chicago Press, 1946.
Weidenreich, F. The Trend of Human Evolution. Evolution, 1 (1947): 4.
Weinmann, J. P., and H. Sicher. Bone and Bones. Fundamentals of Bone Biology. St. Louis: C. V. Mosby Co., 1947.
White, J. C., and T. H. Peterson. Lumbar Herniations of Intervertebral Disks; Value of Surgical Removal for Naval Personnel. Occup. Med., 1 (1946): 145.
Williams, J. W. A Case of Spondylolisthesis with Descriptions of the Pelvis. Trans. Amer. Gynecol. Soc. Phila., XXIV (1899): 49.
Williams, P. C. Lesions of the Lumbosacral Spine: Pt I, II. Journ. Bone Joint Surg., 19 (1937): 343, 690.
Willis, T. A. The Lumbo-sacral Vertebral Column in Man; Its Stability of Form and Function: Amer. Journ. Anat., 32 (1923): 95.
Willis, T. A. The Separate Neural Arch. Journ. Bone Joint Surg., 13 (1931): 709.
Willis, T. A. Backache, an Anatomical Consideration. Journ. Bone Joint Surg., 14 (1932): 267.
Willis, T. A. Anatomical Variations and Roentgenographic Appearances of the Low Back in Relation to Sciatic Pain. Journ. Bone Joint Surg., 23 (1941): 410.
Wood-Jones, F. Arboreal Man. London: E. Arnold, 1916.

www.ingramcontent.com/pod-product-compliance
Lightning Source LLC
Jackson TN
JSHW070314120426
100741JS00007B/59